ENGLISH 3
Spelling, comprehension, imaginative writing

Sandra Soper

**A Piccolo Original
Piccolo Books**

Notes for parents

The aim of this book is to encourage your child to read and write at home. A great deal will be picked up from your attitude to the work, so when you have time, talk with your child about each activity before you start. Children learn a lot from such conversation and because of it, many mistakes and misunderstandings can be avoided. When a mistake does happen, use it as a learning point rather than a reason for criticism. If you are over-critical you could put the child off the work altogether. Praise when you can but when there is obviously a lack of effort, do say so.

At this stage, the child should be practising joined-up handwriting. Your child's school will have a handwriting policy. Find out what it is and use the exercises in this book to practise the school's agreed style. It is very confusing for a child to have conflicting instruction from home and school.

Encourage your child to read aloud, and listen whenever you can. It is a neglected skill, yet such a useful one, which gives confidence, increases understanding, helps pronunciation and adds to enjoyment.

a b c d e f g h i j k l m n o p q r s t u v w x y z

ab cdef ghij klmnop qrstuv wx yz

A B C D E F G H I J K L M N O P Q R S T U V W X Y Z

Read about Midge and answer the questions.

When Lottie and Robert O'Neil first heard that they were to move house because of their father's job, they didn't really believe it would happen. Lottie dreaded the move. She'd lived in the same town since she was born and couldn't imagine life anywhere else. Their parents were naturally anxious about it all. As things turned out they needn't have worried.
The move was a huge success. Both children were given a warm welcome at their new school and, within a few months it was as if they'd been there forever.
One Saturday Mrs O'Neil was driving Rob to his first appointment at the new dentist. 'Hi, Midge,' yelled a lad from across the street. 'Hi Marlon,' Rob waved back.
Mrs O'Neil looked at her son. 'Midge?'
'That's me,' Rob smiled.
'Since when?'
'Oh quite a while'.
Actually the nickname had started at the beginning of term, soon after he joined the class. Tony, one of the more loutish boys, who tended to speak first and think later had said, 'Bit of a midget aren't you? I think we'll call you Midge.'
Rob's reply was brilliant.
'Yeah, great name' he said. Tony was left looking a bit stupid and Rob from that minute was 'O.K.' in the eyes of the others. Somehow the nickname stuck.
Mrs O'Neil didn't think much of the name but she looked on the bright side. 'Oh well, I suppose if you're on nickname terms they must like you.'

....

1   Describe how you would feel if you discovered you had to move to another town.

2   How were the children treated at their new school?

3   Why was Mrs O'Neil surprised when her son replied to Marlon?

4   How did Rob react to Tony calling him a midget?

Read the poem aloud to a partner, then copy it out to practise your handwriting.

Sergeant Brown's Parrot

Many policemen wear upon their shoulders
Cunning little radios. To pass away the time
They talk about the traffic to them, listen to the news,
And it helps them to Keep Down Crime.

But Sergeant Brown, he wears upon his shoulders
A tall green parrot as he's walking up and down.
And all the parrot says is, 'Who's a pretty boy then?'
'I am,' says Sergeant Brown.

Posy Simmonds

All the words below are underline(nouns). underline(Nouns) are words which name things. Tick those which you can see from where you are sitting. Cross out those which you cannot see.

chair	light	fridge	curtain
hand	cupboard	carpet	door
pencil	switch	television	floor
shoe	wall	finger	ceiling
table	arm	cooker	book
window	fish tank	kettle	plant

underline(Adjectives) are words which describe nouns. All the words below are underline(adjectives).

green	wooden	coloured
electric	plastic	plain
gas	white	open
thick	thin	clean
glass	black	painted
small	patterned	dirty

Choose a suitable adjective to go with nine of the words you have ticked and draw a small diagram to make a label.

black shoe				

Here is a description of Midge's kitchen which he wrote for homework. Read it through, then underline the nouns in black and the adjectives in a different colour.

> My kitchen is at the back of the house. It is quite big with one big window and one small one. There is also a window in the door to the garden. There is a wooden table by the big window. Opposite the table sits a big wooden dresser. This usually has a lot of clutter on it. At the far end is the sink with the electric cooker on one side and the washing machine on the other. On the wall above the cooker is a metal plate rack. The walls and ceiling are white and the floor has lino tiles on it. Some of the tiles are chipped and cracked.

Now write a description of your own kitchen.

_____
_____
_____
_____
_____
_____
_____
_____
_____

Read the words, then join each word to the box with the same spelling for the 'u' sound. Write the word again.

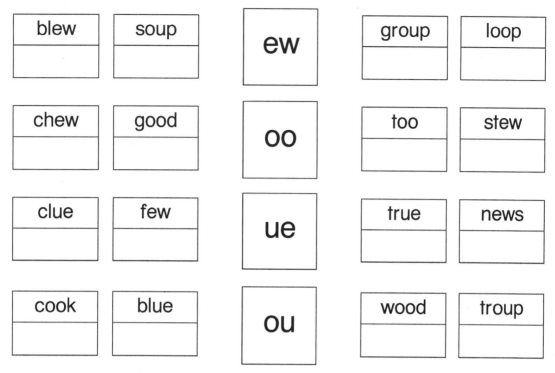

blew	soup		ew		group	loop
chew	good		oo		too	stew
clue	few		ue		true	news
cook	blue		ou		wood	troup

Underline the words from above in these cartoon captions. Colour the pictures.

new shoes

... in the soup...

looping the loop

Too many cooks...

... spoil the broth.

Read the story, then underline the 'u' sounds. (e.g. blue, chew, cool).

'Oh good,' said Lottie. 'Tomato soup, my favourite.'
She and Midge had just come in from school. They both cycled and the journey usually took only a few minutes. Today they were later than usual because they had stopped to watch the big blue lorry from the council cleansing department as it lowered a thick tube into a drain to suck out the contents. They had met Mum in the street on her way home from work and the three of them came in together.
'Lunch in a few minutes,' Dad called from the kitchen. 'Wash your hands while the soup cools.' Then, turning to the cat he said, 'Now you needn't start mewing, you've had yours.'
The children sat at the table. Midge blew some soup over the edge of the bowl.
'Mi..i..dge,' said Lottie, disapprovingly.
'I was only trying to cool it down,' mumbled Midge. 'Miss Goody Two Shoes.'
'It will soon cool,' said Dad. 'Have some celery while you wait.'
Midge chewed a piece of celery while the soup grew cooler.
Soon a group of children were heard at the front door. Midge pushed his chair back.
'I knew it,' he said. 'Now I'll be late.'

Write a word which looks and sounds similar to:

blew	group	look	blue
school	new	full	boot

Lottie wrote a poem about food. First she wrote a list of her favourite foods, then she used this to help her write a poem. Read the list, and draw a picture beside each item.

Apples
Chocolate yoghurt
Fish fingers
Peanut butter
Edam cheese
Flapjacks

Tomato soup
Mayonnaise
Celery
Bananas
Upside down cake
Hard boiled eggs

Read the poem aloud then write an answer to the question.

I like chocolate yoghurt and upside down cake,
I like peanut butter and the flapjacks we bake;
Marmalade and beetroot
I do not like at all but –
Celery with mayonnaise, I like best of all!

Mum says it's odd that I will not eat fish,
Except in fish fingers – a favourite dish.
I used to like spaghetti till Midge* said, 'Mmmm, worms'
Now whenever I see it my poor stomach squirms!
* my brother

What happened to put Lottie off spaghetti?

_____

_____

9

Read the poem on p.9 again and the list of Lottie's favourite foods. Write a list of your own favourite foods, then use it to help you write a food poem of your own.

Rewrite each word sounding out the silent letter, then go over the silent letter in felt pen. Now write the word again from memory.

e.g.

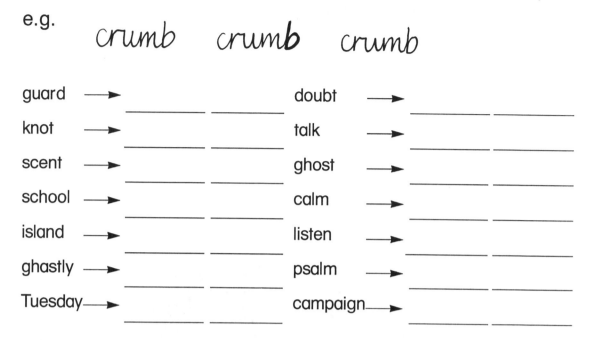

Read through the story first, then underline the words which contain a silent letter.

The litter campaign was started last Tuesday. Mr Andrews announced it to the whole school in Monday's assembly.
'We have a litter crisis,' he'd said. 'The playground is in a ghastly mess. By next Tuesday I want every crumb to have disappeared. This means that we must all be on our guard against the demon litter dropper.'
The children listened calmly. He was always going on about some crisis or other.
'No doubt the problem would soon be sorted out . . .,' Mr Andrews droned on. Lottie began to daydream. She imagined hundreds of litter demons in the shape of garden gnomes darting around the playground emptying dustbins and wastepaper baskets.
Suddenly she was brought back to reality by Petra's voice whispering urgently in her ear. 'C' mon, hymn 67.'

Read the passage, then answer the questions.

Lottie sat down on the grass. She felt hot, tired and thirsty. She had walked all the way up to the den at the top of the hill and there was no one there.
'Be there by one o'clock,' Midge had said. 'And don't forget the food bag. Ask Mum for some extra flapjacks, I think Ken's coming.'
She had managed to get the extra flapjacks and some apples too and had packed them into her lightweight nylon backpack.
The church clock struck one just as she had arrived at the den. There was no sign of anyone there or of anyone having been there recently. It was now half past one and still there was no sign of Midge or Ken. Lottie shivered. It had become suddenly cooler. She had never been at the den all by herself before. And, although she wasn't exactly scared she wished that the others would appear.

'I wonder where they can be?' she asked aloud, as she went to the edge of the path to look down the hill again.

Why was Lottie tired and thirsty?

_____

Whom did she expect to meet at the den?

_____

Why had Midge asked her to bring extra flapjacks

_____

How do we know that she arrived on time at the den?

_____

Invent an ending to the story and write it out on some spare paper.

Read the poem aloud to a partner, then copy it out to practise your handwriting.

January and February
Lean months of the year.
Christmas past, icy blast,
Prospect bleak and drear.

Suddenly a snowdrop
Shows its welcome head,
Conjuring up the thought that
Spring surely lies ahead.

Read the words, then join each one to the box with the same spelling for the 'ow/ou' sound. Write the word again.

out	flour		sour	frown
		ow		
brown	sound		crowd	now

hour	clown		pound	mouth
		ou		
cow	town		loud	allow

Rewrite the words under the proper sound headings to make sensible phrases. Illustrate four of them below.

ou

	wash
	track
self-raising	
	glass
	burst
	coin

ow

dairy	→
circus	→
football	→
up and	→
	hall
	and then

14

Read the story then underline the 'ow/ou sounds, e.g. h<u>ou</u>se, br<u>ow</u>n.

Midge and Lottie were in their way home from school. They each had a bundle of jumble sale notices which they were to deliver to houses in their street. They went home first to drop off their schoolbags and have something to eat. They helped themselves to a couple of brownies each, then went off.
'I'll do the odds, you do the evens, OK?' Lottie nodded. 'Our house first then, she laughed, as she posted a notice through her own front door.
Half an hour later they were finished. As they walked back down the street, Midge counted the notices he had left. 'Now where's that envelope Mrs Baker gave me?' Mrs Baker had said she couldn't come to the sale but would like to make a donation to the school and had given him a small brown envelope. 'I must have posted it through one of the doors,' he frowned, 'but which one?'
Later that evening Mr Brown from down the road came round with the envelope.
'I've just found this with your jumble sale notice,' he laughed. 'I'm sure you didn't mean to give me the donation.' Midge took the envelope.
'Oh, thanks a lot Mr Brown. Now I won't have to go back to all those houses.'

Write a word which looks and sounds similar to:

about	found	proud	our
down	brown	now	shower

All the words below are <u>verbs</u>. <u>Verbs</u> are doing or action words. Tick those words which <u>you</u> can do.

skip	laugh	ski	cycle
breathe	speak	dance	type
walk	drive	swim	sew
draw	blink	fly	skate
whistle	jump	sing	growl

<u>Adverbs</u> are words which describe verbs. All the words below are <u>adverbs</u>.

loudly	carefully	quickly
fiercely	fast	clearly
badly	back	soon
neatly	down	slowly
safely	low	well
high	now	up

Choose suitable adverbs to go with nine of the verbs above, then draw a picture to go with the words.

sing well

16

Here is Lottie's acount of a class outing. Read it through, then underline all the verbs in black and the adverbs in a different colour.

The coach left promptly at 9.30 a.m. We drove slowly till we came to the dual carriageway then the driver picked up speed. We were off to visit Locksley Farm as part of our class project on farm animals. I was chatting to Petra when suddenly I remembered I hadn't taken my travel sickness pill. My heart sank. I went to tell Mr Ledger.
'Oh Lottie' he said crossly. 'You always forget something don't you?' He moved me to the front of the bus and told me to breathe deeply. My Dad once told me to think of daffodils when I felt sick. I thought of them like mad as we drove along. I wasn't sick but I was very glad to get off the coach when we arrived at the farm.
First the farmer showed us two Jacob's sheep, then two new ponies. After that we went round by ourselves. I liked the baby pigs best but the smell in the pigsty was horrible.
Before we went home we were each given a new-laid egg. I gave mine to Petra to hold while I pulled up my sock which had slipped right down into my boot. She was measuring my egg against hers when Daniel Smollick bumped into her. Both eggs smashed. I went to tell Mr Ledger. 'Trust you Lottie. Good thing Mr Beaton gave us a few extra, isn't it?'
I like Mr Ledger but he never sees my side of things.

1. Which adverb tells us that the coach left on time? _____

2. Which verb tells us what Lottie was doing when she remembered her pill. _____

3. Which adverb tells us that Mr Ledger was not pleased with Lottie? _____

4. Which verb and adverb tell us what he told her to do? _____

Write an opposite word at the other end of each arrow, then do p.19.

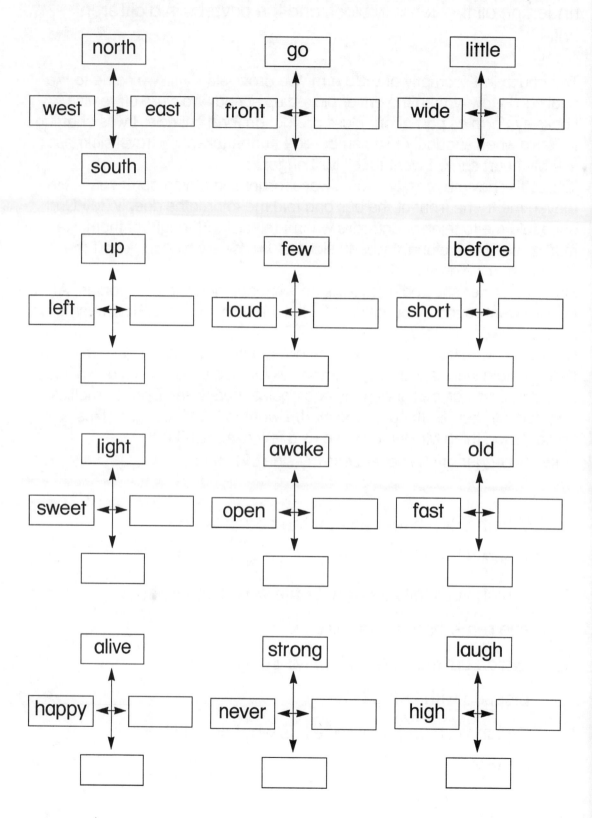

Read the rhymes aloud. Underline the opposites in each one. Choose one of the rhymes to copy out below or make up a rhyme of your own to show a pair of opposites.

Exercise
Nod to the left
Nod to the right
Stretch up, stretch down
With all your might

True or False?
When we're awake
Our eyes are open
When we're asleep
Our eyes are closed
Or are they?

Cheer Up
Laugh and the world laughs with you
Weep and you weep alone

Sick Bed
When I'm ill
My father's a doctor
When not well
My mother's a nurse
Do you think
I want to get better?
When I'm ill
I want to get worse!

The Middle Way
Never
Say never
Never
Say always
Rather say sometimes
For you never know

Love Poem
East West
Home's best
Go by land
Go by sea
At the end
Come home to me

_____

_____

_____

_____

_____

Read the story, then answer the questions on p.21

The local meadow didn't always freeze in the winter. When it did people were quick to take advantage of it. Out came the skates and sledges. Those who had none used tin trays, bits of plastic, washing up bowls, dustbin lids – anything which slid over the ice would do.
This year it had been frozen for most of January. It had been used a lot but was still fine for skating.
The O'Neils had just arrived. Midge was struggling like mad to get his foot into a boot. 'Oh this is no good, it will not go on.' He threw the boot to one side. Lottie was secretly delighted. She'd been longing for ages to have a go on the ice.
'You try them on,' Mum said. Midge kicked at the snow.
'They're fine!' Lottie beamed with pleasure.
'Steady now.' Dad held a hand out to help her up. She wobbled a bit at first but didn't actually fall. Her practice with roller boots probably helped. 'Just like floating on air' she said lifting her arms up.
'How does she know what floating on air feels like?' Midge muttered under his breath.
'For goodness sake,' Mrs O'Neil turned to him. 'It isn't her fault that your feet have grown.'
'Go and get the flask from the car, I'll make a hot drink,' Dad said handing him the keys. Midge trudged off.
On his way, he glanced over the meadow and saw Lottie come down with quite a hard bump. He couldn't have said why but his spirits lifted a little. He straightened his shoulders and his steps quickened towards the car.

Colour Midge's boots

Read the story on p.20 before you answer these questions. Write your answers in sentences.

In which season of the year does this story take place?
_____

What was the problem with Midge's boots?
_____

Why was Lottie secretly delighted?
_____

What else can be used besides skates to slide on ice?
_____

Why do you think Midge pulled on his wellingtons grumpily?
_____

How did Lottie manage with the ice skates?
_____

How do you imagine Midge felt about this?
_____

To finish the story, make up a few sentences about what happened when Midge came back with the flask.
_____
_____

Rearrange these words in alphabetical order, then write a definition for each one in your own words. Use a dictionary if you need to.

geography	telephone	sphere
triumph	nephew	alphabet
photograph	elephant	physician
phantom	pheasant	phone

Use bright felt pen to go over the ph in each word to help you remember the spelling.

alphabet	a set of letters or signs in a given order used in a language.
_____	_____
_____	_____
_____	_____
_____	_____
_____	_____
_____	_____
_____	_____
_____	_____
_____	_____
_____	_____
_____	_____

Read the poem aloud to a partner, then copy it out to practise your handwriting.

The Tortoise

A slow dirty tortoise moved clumsily
                across the page,
His rough skin rasped under the
                heavy shell.
His eyes stared like small black pebbles,
                hard, unwinking
As he reached the soft green lettuce leaf
                his mouth split.
Toothlessly he munched, the leaf gradually
                disappearing.

                Wendy Culling

Lottie and her friend Nasreen wrote a letter of complaint to the presenter of a TV programme. Read the letter, then answer the questions.

> 4 Law Rd.,
> Upton,
> Deefort DDY 5SW
>
> 3rd September 1991
>
> Dear Mr. Andrews,
>
> We are very annoyed about the way girls are treated on your show. You always give the boys a second chance to answer a question. The girls never have this. Also you always make excuses for the boys like, 'That was a hard one Brian!' You never do this for the girls. We are keeping a list to record each time a girl is treated unfairly and we hope to see some improvement in your programme.
>
> Yours sincerely,
> Charlotte O'Neil
> Nasreen Chand

1. When was this letter written?

2. It was written in Nasreen's house. What is her address?

3. Why did the girls write the letter?

4. How do you think Mr Andrews felt when he got the letter?

Read the letter on p. 24 and write a draft reply on a piece of paper. When spellings etc. have been checked, copy it out in clear handwriting below. Address the envelope to Nasreen and write in the cost of a first class stamp.

Read this rhyme aloud then underline all the nouns you find. Start from the kittens then draw the bed, room, house etc, until you have drawn all the nouns listed in the verse.

This is the key of the kingdom
In that kingdom there is a city
In that city there is a street
Off that street there winds a lane
In that lane there is a yard
In that yard there is a house
In that house there waits a room
In that room an empty bed
And on that bed a basket
A basket of **kittens**

Kittens in the basket
Basket on the bed
Bed in the room
Room in the house
House in the yard
Yard in the lane
Lane off the street
Street in the city
City in the kingdom and
This is the key of the kingdom.

Copy the words to help you memorize the spelling. Go over the 'ough' and 'augh' with felt pen, then cover the words with a book. Write out each word again and check the spellings.

naughty	taught	fought
_____	_____	_____
_____	_____	_____
daughter	caught	thought
_____	_____	_____
_____	_____	_____
nought	brought	bought
_____	_____	_____
_____	_____	_____

Look at the pictures then read the captions. Write a caption under each picture. Colour the cartoons.

1 caught red handed	2 I thought I could do it
3 taught a lesson	4 bought in a sale

First rearrange each list of words in alphabetical order then write the words out in the plural form.

Random List	Alphabetical Order	Plural Form
raindrop		
pane		
child		
finger		
bud		
flower		
scent		
bower		
rocket		
astronaut		
watch		
his		
he		
heart		
lamb		
mother		
moment		
leaf		
her		

28

Rewrite the following passages changing them into the plural form.

A raindrop trickles slowly down the window pane. The child, his eyes riveted on the raindrop, traces its path with his finger.

First the bud then the flower. Then the scent to fill the bower.

The rocket was due to take off in ten seconds. The astronaut looked at his watch. He could feel his heart beating as he started to count down. Ten, nine, eight, seven . . .

Lamb, bleating for her mother. Stops for a moment while a leaf goes twirling past her nose.

Read the story about Midge and then add one or two sentences of your own to finish it off.

'Haven't you any homework to do?' Dad called as he saw Midge on his way out of the front door.
'Not much, I'll do it later,' Midge called back.
'Do it first,' Dad said.
'But Dad I said I'd meet Tony and . . .'
'No buts,' Dad interrupted. 'Just get it done and then you can go out. I'll help you with it if you like.'
Midge tutted loudly, then shut the front door. 'No it's all right, I'll do it myself thanks.' He went off upstairs dragging the bag behind him so that it bumped against each step as he went.
Inside his bedroom he sat down heavily on his bed. 'Stupid homework,' he said aloud. 'The Spiders Wedding,' he read the title of the poem as he sat down at his desk. 'The stupid spider's stupid wedding,' he muttered in disgust.
Poetry was not one of Midge's favourite subjects and he never read it for pleasure. 'At least I don't have to make one up,' he thought. He was hopeless at that (or thought he was). Lottie was forever making up rhymes and being praised for them. He couldn't see what was so good about making up silly rhymes. Sighing he picked up his pencil . . .

Here is the poem which was part of Midge's homework. Read it aloud, then answer the questions below.

<u>The Spider's Wedding</u>

I sat on the barn's steps and watched the black spider coming towards me.
I felt like screaming
But I moved aside a little, and the dark creature went up a beam.
It stopped
And turned back
And stared at me, and stared.
It said,
'Move on. My business has nothing to do with you.
I shall stand here until you go.'
So I moved on, looking back over my shoulder to see what it would do.
As it went on, I ran back silently to see.
After a few minutes, back the spider came
Proud now, with an air of arrogance. By his side, walked shyly, another spider.
A new bride.
When they came by me they stood
And stared and stared,
Then they went on.
'Ha. A spider's wedding,' I thought.

June Robinson

Where was the author of the poem when she first saw the spider?

What did the spider seem to be saying when it stopped on the beam?

How would you describe the author's feelings on seeing the spider?

Why was the spider proud when he appeared a second time?

Use some of the words on this page to help you to write a poem about a spider.

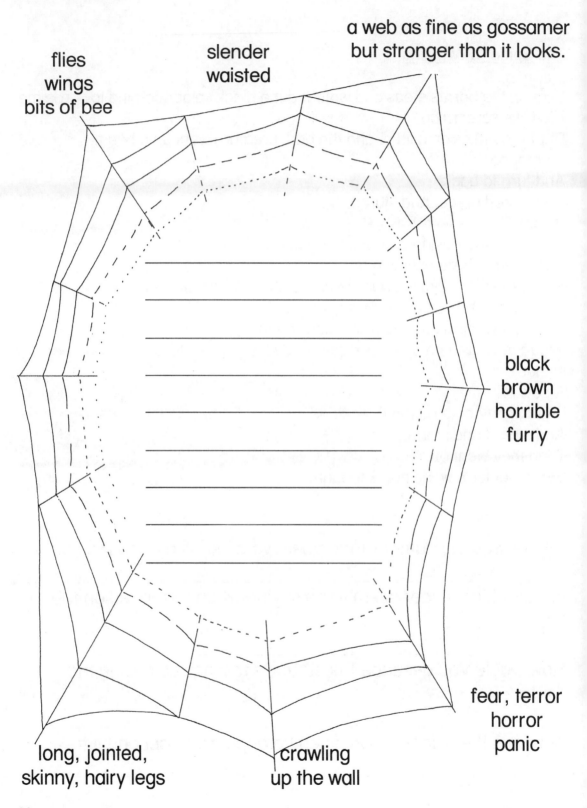

flies
wings
bits of bee

slender waisted

a web as fine as gossamer but stronger than it looks.

black
brown
horrible
furry

fear, terror
horror
panic

long, jointed, skinny, hairy legs

crawling up the wall